The

Destiny Path

Being Alone to Coming Home:
A Heroine's Journey

DIANNA HANKEN

BALBOA.
PRESS

A DIVISION OF HAY HOUSE

Balboa Press books may be ordered through booksellers or by contacting:

Balboa Press
A Division of Hay House
1663 Liberty Drive
Bloomington, IN 47403
www.balboapress.com
1 (877) 407-4847

Because of the dynamic nature of the Internet, any web addresses or links contained in this book may have changed since publication and may no longer be valid. The views expressed in this work are solely those of the author and do not necessarily reflect the views of the publisher, and the publisher hereby disclaims any responsibility for them.

The author of this book does not dispense medical advice or prescribe the use of any technique as a form of treatment for physical, emotional, or medical problems without the advice of a physician, either directly or indirectly. The intent of the author is only to offer information of a general nature to help you in your quest for emotional and spiritual well-being. In the event you use any of the information in this book for yourself, which is your constitutional right, the author and the publisher assume no responsibility for your actions.

Any people depicted in stock imagery provided by Thinkstock are models, and such images are being used for illustrative purposes only. Certain stock imagery © Thinkstock.

Print information available on the last page.

ISBN: 978-1-5043-7988-5 (sc)
ISBN: 978-1-5043-7989-2 (e)

Balboa Press rev. date: 05/19/2017

To Spirit

THE SEASONS OF DESTINY

ACKNOWLEDGEMENTS

To all the angels on my path:

My teachers and coaches Jean, Claire, Heide, Ashley, Sara, Richard, and Craig;

My cousin Lauren, my brother Scott, and beloved friends Reyna, Dixie, and Nina;

My West Coast and East Coast families, including the DeFino clan;

My dear sisters in the tribe, with special appreciation to Alicia, Bonnie, Cheri, Danielle, Ellie, Jeanette, Julia, Katie, Maggie, Meredith, and Sandy;

My precious boys, Nolan and Ethan. They have seen their Momma transform into a completely new person, and if it was ever scary for them, they hid it well. They are so over me talking about Spirit, but I still drop it into conversation on occasion. They are brilliant, shining lights, and I treasure their hugs and kisses;

And finally, to the musicians who are sharing their stories and singing their gifts. I never knew until recently there were songs that spoke my soul and to all that I knew was possible. The music kept me grounded as I flew into the stars, and the voices that sang of what I knew to be true made me cry, laugh, sing, dance, and smile.

I am forever grateful to all of you.

EARLY WINTER

Tuning Into Desire

"'Cause every one of us has a purpose here,
sometimes it's hidden underneath your fear. Just
takes some time for the truth to come out."

— "Courage to Grow," by Rebelution

I was alone. I had always had this feeling since I can remember.
And even though I was seen as friendly, outgoing and personable,
inside I was dying. Always feeling like I didn't fit in, or that people
didn't understand me. Or essentially that I didn't even matter.
My family didn't really know me, nor did my husband. And I
certainly didn't choose friends that did.

On the outside, it all seemed to be going well. I was raised in
a two-parent household, had three siblings, married a guy I met
in college, had no debt, had a successful career selling real estate,
had no problems getting pregnant, had two beautiful boys, and
traveled. There were long stretches in my life where I was "happy."
I am a serial optimist, so I made the best out of everything. The

grass wasn't greener on the other side, so I did what I had to do even when those moments of, "I just want to be heard and seen and known" would pop into my head. I would quickly dismiss those thoughts and carry on. Because really, what did I have to complain about? I did have a good life compared to the majority of people in this world. So what if I was never fully known to the depths of my soul? I could shut that piece out and keep going – because, you see, I didn't know it could be any different.

I have always been a spiritual person. I was raised Catholic, and I remember as a kid being at church and talking to God, but dismissing the whole Mass part, the boring sermons and the long standing. But at the same time I felt connected to something, so I tolerated it. I got married in the Catholic church and looked forward to those times in the year when I could plan meals and gatherings around the religious holidays.

Others might have seen me as a good Catholic, and I did connect to the rhythms and the structure of the traditions. What I didn't connect to was the politics and masculine dominance of the Church, and I know now that was Spirit protecting me and leading me home even in those days. My husband was not religious, so I would do all these things alone (no surprise there! You'll see a theme), but I didn't mind, or at least I didn't think I did. I was good at doing things alone, not asking for help, and being independent. I am an optimist and knew that I could control my own joy and destiny, so what better way to do that than to do what made me happy. And hence ran the pattern of my life.

It is difficult to know how this pattern of aloneness really began to take shape. Of course in childhood, but from whom did I acquire this? Did anyone in my family model it? I am not sure, but I can define some scenarios that created who I became. My mother was a stay-at-home mom and had four children. I was the third child with a 9-year gap between my youngest sister and me, so I was the baby for a while before she came along. I remember playing by myself much of the time. My two older siblings were 5 and 6 years older than me, and because they always hung out together, I was essentially on my own. Not only that, the older two would incessantly pick on me, so even though my heart ached to be a part of what they were doing, I was shut out over and over again. My mother didn't play with me as she was too busy taking care of the cooking, cleaning, and shopping, so she didn't have much time or energy left over for recreation. Don't get me wrong, though. I did get hugs and kisses, there was no abuse, we had a little bit of money, and I was always fed, so again, on the grand scale, I had it pretty good.

But this pattern of wanting to be a part of something and not fully connecting transferred into my friendships as well. I never had a best friend. I had a couple of girls in the neighborhood who I would play with, but I didn't feel like I truly belonged. I would desperately want to play with them, but when I did, I would do what they wanted to do, go with their suggestions and many times be a doormat because I wanted to be included so desperately. I also didn't fit in at school and was teased a lot. I didn't have the "right" clothes or the looks that the guys apparently liked. I was fairly smart and got good grades, but wasn't the best at anything.

What I did have was music. I learned to play the piano and loved to sing. Again, neither spectacularly, but it brought me home to myself, although at the time I just knew it to make me happy. In middle school I was in show choir and had a knack for learning music quickly, and loved to dance with the songs. I became a leader in this arena and it was my favorite class. I continued with singing and dancing in high school and in the pattern that would continue throughout my life, I became a leader while not fitting in all the way. Part of me kept it all separate, so even though I could lead the choir and run a rehearsal, others probably feared me more than wanted to hang out with me.

The river of love moving through me never stopped. It would just constantly get diverted and dammed to hold back, never fully trusting anyone, and the love stopped flowing as freely. My heart, little by little, shut down. I felt so much and loved so deeply that after a while, it was so much easier to control it all than to let it just run its course and feel the pain.

I had no modeling to show me how to keep my heart open. I was told I was too sensitive, not to cry so much, so I became strong instead. I had to learn to put up armor to protect myself in my family. Knowing or caring about feelings and emotions wasn't even in the ballgame.

Walls of protection don't happen overnight. I can look back and see how much I wanted to be loved for who I really was, but the choices I would continually make would lead me to not feel valued. The friends that would want to be friends with me, well, I had no interest in them. If they started to want me, I would push them away. It would make me feel uncomfortable. And then I would choose the friends who weren't all the way there, who would play with me if they didn't have something better to do or if they wanted to run the show. I was so deep and wide and open, but after a while, the river became smaller and didn't rush as big and wide as it once did before.

Pain. Heart-felt pain. Oh, how uncomfortable you are! How you make me want to run and hide. I know you, pain, so true and visceral it makes me turn the other way. How was I to recognize you for who you truly were? A guidepost, my lover, my friend. I did not learn to know you, so whenever I would meet you, I would run. Like all the other patterns in my life, if it didn't make me happy or comfortable, I would just switch my attention to something else. I have learned to come towards you and feel you, and I cry with the knowing of your wisdom and your infinite capacity to show me love. You rained down on me like a storm; however, because you needed me to pay attention, and because I was so used to going the other way, you had to wake me up from the deep sleep of not feeling. But you were my marker along the way to give me the right direction. And so all my years of running and stopping the flow brought me back to you.

Some people may call it God, Universe, or nature. I love the word Spirit, so that is what I use. Spirit to me encompasses the divinity of where we come from and ultimately what we go back to. Never-ending, ever-expanding, infinite love. Divine. It was always with me even when I was systematically shutting down my heart. But it's always been strong. When I would go to church, I would feel a connection, but it wasn't the type of flowing connection that I knew was possible. But I stayed with the church because it was where I felt most home. I knew it wasn't truly home, but it was close enough. Everything was always just close enough.

Then one day the tide started to turn. Of course I didn't know it at the time, but the reversal of flow started to happen. It was small cracks in the dam and pain was there to meet me. I wasn't happy. Despite trying in my perfectionistic way to do it all right, and do more and more and more to make it all happen, I was exhausted. Spirit gave me an experience of breaking my foot to try and slow me down, and I had an inkling that was what was happening, but I still kept moving. I mulled over the thought to rest more, but the momentum of how I was going was still too strong. I had a dream of my beloved making love to me in the most exquisite, orgasmic, spiritual way, and I woke up from the dream desperately hanging on to that feeling but so depressed knowing I would never have it as my husband who never touched me lay next to me. Spirit was trying to show me the way – come home!

This way of being for me – strong, independent, never asking for help – brought many gifts. I would need this inner strength to get me through what I was going to have to endure. From the outside, it was a divorce, a company job change, a new house, and a new way of showing up in my life. But how could anyone know the mountains I had to move internally to get there? I would rarely express my unhappiness, and even when I did, it was met with others knowing more than me, knowing the life path better, or it was met with fear because I wasn't fitting into the container they knew me to be. This was not the positive, happy Dianna they knew, so they would turn away. I wasn't meant to show my pain or unhappiness because then it was a reminder to them of their unmet pain. But I had the courage to go the distance, and in doing so, I would be able to shift lifetimes of patterns that were ready to be discarded.

WINTER

Embracing It All

"If it was up to me, I'd teach that the loneliness
is just part of the courage it takes."

— Nahko

It's funny to me how life will come at you in one direction to get you to move in another. In my desperation to fit in and be a part, I was nice. As is typical for females, I wanted to be liked, but my aloneness would keep me from really being a part of things. So if I were to guess, others probably saw me as friendly but aloof. My boys were in a private school, and it was a tight-knit community. I took a relatively active part, chatted with other moms, went on field trips, picked my boys up from school (all of this, of course, while working full-time as a realtor, cooking all the family meals, etc. Overachiever!!). I was having issues with my older son being nice and fitting in, and that took up a good deal of my mental energy. I needed him to behave! I needed him to be nice! This didn't fit into my pattern!! So imagine my surprise when my younger son, who was being bullied most of the year, pushed another kid at the water fountain and chipped his tooth. Oh, the internal horror I was going through! Why couldn't they just fit in? I was in inner hell and turmoil. It started to spiral out of control. My son apologized, but the other mother wasn't happy. She was aggressive and got in my face, and I told her I didn't want to talk to her. She raged, started gossip about my kids and me throughout the school, and even went to the board to have us removed from the school. All the while, I just wanted to not be seen, have it all go away, and for my kids to just fit in. I meditated for hours at a time. I was in so much pain that meditating was the only place I could go to get any relief. My husband, who could listen to my angst for 10 minutes at a time, did nothing. I was strong, and he hated conflict, so it was left to me to handle.

Every one of these challenges were blessings. How could I see at the time the absolute perfection in all of this? If I had a different partner, I wouldn't have had to deal with it on my own and learn my inner strength. If I didn't have a mother who knew all the answers and couldn't hear and support me, I wouldn't have had to go within. Every single piece of everything in our lives is at such perfection that it brings me to a place of awe.

This situation at the school went on for months until the end of the school year. In the end, we stayed, and the other family left. It was the biggest catalyst in my life that got me turned around. Because of my pattern of being alone, I went inward. I was always a meditator, and I would meditate once a day for around 30 minutes. Now I meditated for hours on end because I was so unhappy. I knew that I had to figure out why. I then took the first step in changing the direction of my life – I reached out for help.

I sought out an Ayurvedic teacher, and he and I had a few

sessions. I cried like never before. I didn't know it at the time, but he was opening my heart. I had so many angels along the way. I went to see Braco the healer when he was in town, and he opened my heart some more. Tears and tears and tears. All the while I was raising two small boys, being a wife, keeping the household running, and working.

Then, exhaustion set in. I could barely function. My body was starting to shut down. I started to have severe heart palpitations. I reached out to an energy healer my Ayurvedic teacher suggested, and the issue was my thyroid. It was maxed out and starting not to function. She gave me some herbs to help me heal and told me how much my husband loved me. I decided to stick it out and see if I could make the marriage work. I had to get to a place inside of me where I knew my own happiness lay. At that point I could make the decisions I knew I had the courage to make. I intuitively knew I wasn't there yet, though. So I kept at it.

Around this time an email for a personal growth course hit my inbox. At this point, I had never done any "self-help" classes. So the first time this email came through, I deleted it. And then again. And again. I didn't know why I was on that mailing list. By the fourth time or so, I opened it. It was a nine-week Integral Enlightenment online course. I really didn't even know what that was, but I felt drawn to take it, so I did. I don't even remember what it taught, but when it was over, I took the next 11-week course that followed. I don't remember what was taught in that one either.

But these courses were starting to connect me back to myself. Like a flower that is opening, each layer that was being removed from my heart would open up a petal. It was slow, and so painful, but the tides were so strong pulling me there I couldn't stop it. I was on the banks of the shore trying to hold on sometimes, but the current would keep yanking me back in. I really didn't have a choice. My soul knew it was going home, and it would continue to take me there. I was just the body trying to hang on, and my ego was desperate, but the current kept moving.

Then these courses led me to a seven-week Feminine Power course. Now, this got me excited. I didn't know why, but this completely captured my attention. *What's an inner glass ceiling?* I was starting to get the sense that I had a fairly powerful intuition, and boy, I had no idea! During this course there would be women who would call in and ask questions, but I didn't remember ever doing that. I was used to doing everything by myself, so why would I ask for help? Plus, I would get annoyed at the women who would go on and on with their questions. Just get to the point already! *"How can they talk that much?"* would scream my lovely alone inner self.

I know I had many breakdowns to breakthroughs during these first couple of years of transformation, but the first one I really remember was during this Feminine Power course. The instructor led us through an exercise of going within and naming old patterns. Once we could see it and name it, we could then release it. Mine was around being invisible. It was a powerful experience for me! The rest of the course went along mostly uneventful, but that was my first experience with Feminine Power and all the gifts it would hold for me.

Since I was on a roll with all these online courses (and funny, actually. This fit in so well with my being-alone scenario! How great that I could do all these courses by myself, down in my basement, alone! If I missed a live session, I could just listen to the recordings later. Brilliant! How terrific to be able to figure myself out all by myself. It was perfection), I decided to take an 11-month Jean Houston Quantum Destiny course.

Now again, put this all in perspective. I was not one to do any self-help, spirituality stuff. The thought actually turned me off. But Spirit and intuition were always leading me, and even though I didn't know it, they were always guiding me. I didn't need any of it until I did, and then when I did, I could follow where I needed to go. My mind and ego weren't filled with all the "knowledge" of knowing it all, so when it was time, I was able to go in the direction I needed to without having to break through all the supposedly gained wisdom I already had.

So in stepped my next teacher, Jean. I had vaguely heard of her before although she's been around for decades and written probably 30 books. This is the part of the story that gets interesting. We were going to learn how to use the quantum realm to tap into our higher potentials. Guess what is a key factor to getting up there? Music. Right up my alley. Another factor is imagination: Being alone a lot, I had cultivated a pretty good one. A third factor is a strong sense of spirit. By this time, I knew what was guiding me, and it wasn't me! And although it wasn't specifically stated, the courage to let go. The slow opening of my heart, the hours of meditation, was prepping me all for this.

I am not even sure how it happened, or exactly when it did, but as crazy as it sounds, Jean taught me how to jump worlds. The first few months of the course laid down the foundation, and again, I am not even sure how it all happened. But then after that, it all kicked into high gear. Remember how I used to meditate for hours? Well, that was a quiet affair. I could sit pretty much anywhere, close my eyes, and just be gone. No movement of my body, and it all seemed pretty peaceful. Well, not anymore. I had to lay down flat on my bed because the energy moving through me was so powerful. My whole body was shaking, my head moved side to side at rapid speed. I had no idea what was happening to me! But I also knew it was all okay. I didn't fear it.

It was an interesting phenomena. My kids said I was doing the convulsion thing again. Then after a few weeks my eyes got into it. They started to flutter, roll back into my head, but again, no fear. I knew it was okay. It was through this training that I learned to instantly connect with the Spiritual realm. What I realized later was that I was literally transforming every cell in my body. My brain was being reformatted with such intense energy, and that is why I had to lie down. A teacher at Jean's workshop later in the summer would tell me that I was learning to reality surf. It is a very high level of conscious awareness. All I can say is, how freaking cool is that?!

So now new patterns were emerging in my life. The river was opening back up within me. I decided to leave my marriage of over 20 years. I went into it not feeling worthy and being alone, and although he was a good and decent person, our time together was over. I can't tell you what courage it took for me to speak the words, but we both knew it was finished. There were no arguments, no discussions. Just, "I can't do this anymore," from me and an "Okay" from him. He never wanted to hurt me, and I believe he was waiting on me to call it off because of that. Whatever the reason, we both knew it was done.

SPRING

Becoming Spirit-Led

"Everything that's new to me is an opportunity.
So I'm gonna grow, and you can grow, too."

— Satsang

There have been many, many angels on my journey and path, and I couldn't have gotten to where I am without them. But three have been most significant. The first was Jean, who taught me how to connect with Spirit in the most divine way for me. I attended an eight-day workshop with her, and being with Jean and the participants, I learned that what I had done was not unusual at all, and in fact, most people in that room had been going into different Universes their whole lives. I was a newcomer to this realm, but I was finally home in that sense. The second teacher was Claire Zammit, the founder of Feminine Power. Remember that seven-week course I had taken previously? Well, while I was taking Jean's course, I signed up for the nine-month Feminine

Power Mastery course. It started in January, right around the time my whole mind was being recalibrated.

There are four "prongs" to being a grounded, enlightened being in my mind. It is up and down and side to side. The up and down is connection to Spirit (above) and the grounding into Mother Earth (below). Jean taught me that. The third and fourth prongs, side to side, is connection with yourself and your connection with others. You have to know how to live in community with yourself, in its true form, and learn how to live in relationship with others. If one of the four pieces is missing, you won't be complete. And none of them are destinations. We are spiritual beings having a human experience, so we will never get there. But it's the journey and the discoveries along the way that make this life worth living.

Claire and her team and teachings taught me where to begin on the inside. As Jean taught me to go out and connect with the outer, Spiritual world, Claire led me on the inner journey. Feminine Power is all about going within, feeling the feelings, moving from the deep sense of trust and knowing of yourself. The seven-week course was just a taste of what was to open up inside of me and integrate into new ways of showing up in my life. I learned that women have three internal power centers, and by utilizing these centers of power within ourselves, we can break down barriers and can move in a more empowered, authentic way.

At the beginning of the course, we were asked to set an intention for what we wanted to create, expand, or discover over the next nine months. I set two intentions: To call in my Beloved and to determine my destiny/life purpose. Looking back, I didn't really know what I was getting myself into. All I knew was that I had this deep sense of knowing that I was here on the Earth in this particular time and space for something much greater than I could know for myself. What I was meant to do with my life was bigger than I could imagine, and it wasn't selling houses any more. I also knew I could have this beloved in my life where I was seen, met, and known like never before although I have never experienced anything like that except in my dream years ago. So because of the beautiful support of life and the intentions that I set, it started to give me what I wanted. Oh, but not in any way I expected.

The first significant breakthrough came in February. I had just dated a guy for a few weeks, and we were not together anymore. It wasn't right, and I knew it, but I couldn't shake it off. So I asked Spirit, "What am I to learn from this?" The answer came through the next morning as, "self-worth." I was coaching with a beautiful teacher, Ashley, and with her help, I realized I had an issue with self-worth. But not just a little issue. This was a mountain within, and it moved. Not all the way, but a big piece of it, and I now had awareness around this.

A side note on awareness. I have learned that in this opening up to Spirit and the higher realm, awareness is what brings in the learning and teachings. Awareness is what leads you in the right direction. You need to develop trust, and trust comes through your intuition. Then this intuition brings you to places of being aware. But you have to have all three – trusting your intuition to bring in the awareness.

The next significant piece was connecting with my beloved in April. As part of the Mastery course, there was a side course called the Art of Love series. In this, I reached out a golden chord into the realm to connect with my beloved, and we did instantly! It was this incredible flow of love like I had never known before. I cried more tears as I started to experience this unconditional, divine love that I always knew was possible but had never experienced. Although my beloved was not in manifest form on the Earth plane yet, I knew our hearts were connected. Over the next few months I started to speak with him, and he would answer me. It wasn't a voice per se that I heard, but it was words and a knowing. I know – it sounds absolutely impossible and crazy, and trust me when I say I thought I was crazy for a while too. Don't forget I was still on my bed every day for hours in meditation with energy moving so fast through me, still not entirely sure what was going on. I was learning how to reconnect with myself through Feminine Power, being coached, and breaking down inner barriers.

SUMMER

Trusting The Flow

"Love letters to God. I wonder if she reads
them or if they get lost in the stars?"

— Nahko

So this was my summer. High-level meditations, taking the Feminine Power courses every week, being coached, working through inner issues, and connecting significantly with my beloved. I had asked my love to find me through the music, and so he did. I would play music through my iPod, and he would stop me when a song came on and say, "pay attention." And the particular song or the next line in the song would be for me. There is significant meaning to this, and it is based all around trust. There are many moments in our lives where something comes through to us, or into us, or we get this knowing. And we say to ourselves – *That is crazy! Is it real? I'm not going to follow that,* and so we let it go, and we don't follow it. These months, and when these situations would happen, I would say the same thing to myself. And what I had to learn to do was trust. I knew with every fiber of my being that what was happening was real, and so I had to trust. And in that trust, every time I would allow it to come through, my heart would open just a little bit more. The love would pour through. There was so much pain – I was separated, selling my house, building a new home, learning to be on my own again (although I was alone, I was starting to feel less alone), and raising my boys, with no support from my family. Everything was being deconstructed so that it could be reconstructed, and I had to learn how to truly trust the process.

In August, I went to the eight-day training with Jean Houston. This was my first spiritual growth retreat or conference that I had ever attended. I was showing up in different ways, willing to put myself in new and different situations, and being in that space with others who were also on the path was pushing my edge completely. George, as I was now calling my beloved, was there so significantly. Lines of songs would come through and he would say, *This is for you:* "There are eyes, they watch us closely. And there's a story they will tell." (Nahko). This love that was radiating through me was seen by many of the participants, and I was met with affirmation of what I was feeling and creating. It was at this retreat that I was told of my reality surfing, and I then owned my high level of consciousness. All those months of head-shaking and body movement came together. Music was the way we got to the outer realms, and I was now a pro at it. Those days with Jean and her team were a brilliant leap for me. Many things came together, although I had still had so many questions.

FALL

Following Intuition

"So which wolf will you feed? One makes you
strong, one makes you weak. And those who
know, and those who seek, amidst the chaos, find
your peace. I know which wolf I will feed."

— Nahko

Then the Feminine Power retreat came in September. It was nine
days in Berkeley, California, and we were asked to set an intention
for that as well. We were at the end of our nine months in the
Mastery program, and in June I had signed up to train to be a
Feminine Power coach, facilitator, and leader. So the days would
be spent in deep dives around the trainings, and also a celebration
for the end of Mastery. The intention I had set for Mastery to
find my destiny? Well, that was to be a coach and facilitator
in Feminine Power and transformational learning. I knew that
is where I wanted to spend the next half of my life. And these

trainings were another example of perfect and right timing from the Universe.

My main intention for the retreat was to make deep connections with my sisters. I had not met any of them in person yet although we spoke on calls three times a week. I was starting to learn what it was like to be seen and heard by others in a way I never thought possible. And boy, was I met with such incredible grace, love and support! The retreat was unlike anything I had ever experienced. Sisters reflected back to me my brilliance, the light and love they saw within me, and I did the same for them. I had found my tribe!! I was with women and in a community I didn't even know could exist, and my heart opened to even greater depths. I walked out of the retreat feeling on fire with what I was here to do, owning my gifts and wisdom, and having made deep connections with many sisters that I would take with me and continue to cultivate over the next months.

I also continued to have deep, deep connections with George in general and at the retreat. As a test, I asked him to send me flowers seeing how he would manage that. After a couple of days, as I was running along the bay in Berkeley, he turned my head, and along the path I saw exquisite wildflowers blooming on the side of the path that I had not seen before. My heart broke open a little bit more. Other sisters saw his energy right next to me, and he was there whenever I said his name, right over my right shoulder. I felt his presence so deeply and was continuing to trust we would be together one day, hopefully soon. He told me one afternoon how proud he was of me and what an anchor I was becoming. Being that I was looking out at the Marina and the boats, the analogy was not lost on me.

But as had been my journey, and what I had not fully learned yet, is that suffering and pain is a significant part of growth. I had been a very good student – I was trusting, learning, opening, and taking everything that was being thrown at me and moving mountains within. I knew that life never throws at you what you can't handle, but I never knew the dam was about to break open. I thought I had removed enough and had done such significant work that I would have rapids in the river to navigate; but no, the flood was about to happen.

The very next day after I returned home from the retreat (feeling on such a high!), I got hit with a cosmic 2x4. I am not perfect, and in my process of opening my heart, I had gone down a dark path. As is everything that is perfect, however, this experience gave me lifetimes of insight into judgement of myself and others. It was a lesson not to be missed. I had such shame, guilt, judgement, and grief come pouring out of me. My dear coach Ashley was my anchor at the time and she coached me through many hours of turmoil. But the blessing was how fast I moved through it all! It was a couple weeks of intensity, but the grace of Spirit led me through, and the flood had to happen. It had to be cleared, and in the end I had let most of it go.

The next significant torrent that came was the process around George. My boys and I moved into our new home that I had built at the end of October. But George did not come with me. The energy was completely off, and I wasn't feeling him anymore. No more songs, no more coming when I called his name. What was happening? Where was my Beloved? So in came my third and significant teacher.

WINTER

Navigating Next Steps

"And it definitely matters how you look at it. So if you think you can risk it, well, what an opportunity to be free of it."

— Nahko

Heide is a Spiritual Alchemist who is also a coach. I had received her name from a sister who I had connected with at the retreat, and she had done many sessions with her. The whole idea of not needing a coach or help or doing it on my own was so out the window at this point. When George went away, I asked Spirit, *what next?* It answered, *speak to Heide.* So I set a session with her. As are all of us, she is an angel from God. My first question to her was, "Is George who I think he is?" She said no, he's not. He is not my manifest beloved that I have been waiting for. He is not going to appear at my door or on the street or sit next to me on the airplane.

I was on the floor. I couldn't believe it! So what was all that we had shared? I knew that I was not crazy – I trusted that completely – and the love we had exchanged and shared was true and real. The songs he had sent, everything, what was this all about?

The rest of the hour-long session we had was a bit of a blur. We talked about many things and I took some notes, but I was still reeling with this new reality. I cried and cried and cried. I went downstairs, made the boys their dinner, got them into bed, and then fell asleep exhausted. At 2:00 in the morning Spirit woke me, and it all came through so clear. The love that we shared was absolute and real, but it was the idea of it being attached to a *person* that I needed to let go of. All we are is love, and that is all we will ever be, so let go of the idea of it being attached to "George" or "Steve" or "Mary." I could understand that, but still needed more answers. So I asked Spirit, *what next?* It told me to email Jean. So I did. I asked her, "What was I connected to? Was it a twin flame? Spiritual Beloved? What?" She emailed me back and said to read her book, *The Search for the Beloved.*

I went right out and got the book, and it took me a couple days to read it. This is because every other page I said, "Oh, my God!" I couldn't believe it. Everything she was saying was what happened to me. I had connected with my Spiritual Beloved! Here was my intention to connect with my beloved, and I am thinking my physical, Earth-plane partner. Well, instead Spirit had other, better plans for me. What I needed to feel and know was the infinite love of the divine, Spiritual Beloved. That is what continued to open up my heart. No physical person could ever have matched that divine love that I so desperately needed to experience. Talk about a blessing, but not in the way I ever, ever could have imagined.

So yes, I was thrilled with this knowledge, but my ego would not let me go. Ah, beautiful ego. I still wanted this partner who is with me on this lifetime journey, who was sitting next to me on the couch, sharing my bed, holding my hand. So where was that? I wanted this! This was not too much to ask for. I had been an excellent student. I had shed layer after layer, opened up the river, and I was flowing and trusting and letting go at a rate that was almost inhuman. This was the one thing I had wanted, and I was still alone. Alone. Alone.

There was a desperation in my heart. I had another session with Heide. She connected with Spirit, and it worked through her as I learned I would also do. She helped me clear past life issues, judgements I had carried since the time of Christ, and taught me how to truly live with an open heart. Everything had been a step, one step closer to being this open-hearted creature who allowed the pain to flow through while also the joy and bliss of life. Learning how to love my family in the midst of all the pain, how to continue to anchor into my knowing and brilliance and gifts. And in our many sessions she showed me that to have what I want – this Beloved I so wanted – I had to be so anchored within myself, in my self-love and worth, that I would be okay being alone the rest of my life. Oh, that was *so* not easy to hear!

And then in walked a potential partner. This was in December, and I had started to look at him differently. He would send me love when I saw him, but I found I couldn't receive it. Wow – this was fascinating! It was scary for me to receive this love. He worked at a grocery store I frequented, and this played out for about a month. We connected when I was in the store, but nothing happened. He didn't ask for my number, nor did we go out. Just this interplay of something happening. I asked Spirit what next, and it took me to a book – *The Queen's Code* by Alison Armstrong.

I had to learn how to be a brilliant receiver of love. At this point in my journey, I didn't see it as work. Heide helped me see that. It's the journey, not the destination. I had been such the overachiever, perfectionist, do-it-right type of person, that this was a change. I was learning to trust and flow. I was starting to enjoy the experiences. Even with this longing to have someone in my life, I was starting to ride the rapids of change with little drama. They were little rapids now and didn't drag me under.

Then, the morning of January 17th, I was awoken at 4:00 in the morning by Spirit. Because of this learning to love myself and most significantly to receive it, the completion of my being alone was done. It was complete. It came through so clear, and my heart opened up wide. I now chose partnership, I now chose relationship. I will never forget that day and the completion of being alone. As is everything with perfect and right timing, this could not have come without all the steps before. I needed to learn how to let go, trust, and to become a brilliant receiver of love.

Then shortly after, the guy at the grocery store asked for my number, and the next week we were set for a date. I was so excited! He was an example of who I wanted. He was spiritual, a beautiful writer, and he had already given me so many gifts in opening my heart. He had shown me that I needed to learn how to receive love. And I knew that if it went no further than this, he had already given me so much. And it didn't go any further. He stood me up on the date, sending me a text 15 minutes after he should be there to say he couldn't make it, he wasn't ready for a relationship, still working through some loss, and he was so sorry to get me caught up in his mess. I was in shock. I left the bar, went home, sent him a text back and wished him well on his journey, and crawled into bed. Strangely, I was okay. I was learning to trust and flow.

That was a Thursday. The following Wednesday, it all came out. Rage. Anger. So. Much. Anger. I was downstairs in my basement screaming. I was yelling at Spirit that I was done. That's it. It could take this f-ing journey and all that it had in store for me and go on its way. I was not going to coach people or facilitate or listen to it anymore. Done. And this lasted for two days. It all came out – anger with my family, my marriage, George, life, everything!

And then the storm passed. I came back to center and was on course again. Of everything that I had experienced, learned, felt, this was the most significant piece. Why? Because I had learned to love myself enough to feel the anger. We are not taught any of these life lessons – how to live with pain, to process it. And we certainly are not taught how to face and feel our anger. It doesn't exist. If it arises, we stamp it down, push it aside, eat it away, video-game it away, you name it. We don't own it, we don't love it, we don't accept it. And what we need to learn to do is love it. And in this process of it all coming out at once, I was blessed because I realized Spirit knew I could handle it now. It was another part of me that had integrated, and I was filled with gratitude.

February came around and it was time for our final Feminine Power retreat once again in Berkeley. We were a couple months out from completing our coaching and facilitation training, and I was filled with energy and love upon seeing my sisters again and being with the tribe. This was a place of home for me, and it filled me up.

A key piece in Feminine Power is working with the Identity Matrix and knowing our core ones, and mine is, "I'm alone."

There are others such as "I'm not enough" and "I'm invisible," but "I'm alone" has been mine to hold for this entire lifetime, possibly past lifetimes as well. But I didn't fully own that until this retreat. How this feeling of alone had shown up in my life was by feeling like I was not with my people, rarely asking for support, and having a deep sense of sadness by not being connected with others. I was alone in my marriage for 20 years; I had friends but not truly deep friendships, and I had a feeling I wouldn't fully be able to bring my gifts to the world. But the pattern had been shifting. Since September and the first retreat, I had found my tribe, I was making deep connections, I had been learning to connect with myself and others, and I was starting to bring my gifts into the world to be shared. And by learning to love myself even more every day, I kept opening my heart to all that was possible and mine to receive. I left the retreat fully grounded in the knowing of, "I Belong and I am Enough." Even if all of the sisters in the tribe disappeared tomorrow, I knew in my essence that I was not alone. I am so part of this exquisite Universe. I am a drop in the Ocean, and I am the Ocean. All that I am and ever will be is this flow of love expanding and contracting, expanding again into divinity.

SPRING

YOU, Complete Exactly As You Are

"Angels speak of a thing called bliss. Close
your eyes, all we've got is this."

— Trevor Hall

March arrives, and the boys and I go to the island of my heart –
Maui. The sun, sand, and ocean call on my archetype, Aphrodite,
and I am in love with this place all over again. I am feeling open
to what may occur, but I am always on the look-out for him.
Fundamentally, it is still what I desire. I could not have imagined
the journey that has taken me to where I am in this moment in
time. Four or five years ago when it all began, that first time I
started to let my heart open, well, I couldn't be more proud of
where I am standing today. I am in flow and trust, and although
it is not in perfection, it won't ever be. Heide has coached me on
letting my heart open and he will come, and although I trust it, I
still am wanting it. So there is still an edge on where I am going
and what I am desiring.

The first week I am on the island, my energy keeps going out. I am in constant mode of looking at most every guy saying, "Is it him? Is it him?" Not only is it ridiculous, it is crazy! I can't even laugh at it, it is so ridiculous. It makes me angry that I can't pull my energy back to myself. I keep trying to clear myself but nothing seems to be working. Finally, I have enough and call Heide for a short session. I need her help to bring me back to center. After a half-hour session, I feel myself back to center and letting the light flow through me again. The next morning, Spirit wakes me early and I have a massive amount of clearing and self-love. I spend a couple of hours riding the waves of love, and I am grateful.

And then it happens. Around 6:00 in the morning I look at my phone and there is an email. The subject line is "The Sun Is Always Shining," and it is from an instructor who teaches meditation. The title of the email is not lost on me as I sit on the balcony watching the sun rise over the mountains on the island that I love so much. He talks about how he kept trying so hard to always have "that experience" of awakening. He would work harder at it to make it last until he discovered he didn't have to try anymore. Everything was already perfect, and he was already there. And I realized the same thing. I was done trying. I was done working at this. I Am. In truly letting it all go, everything inside me opened up. Everything. I have practiced enough, and I am perfectly perfect in my imperfection. And the most incredible thing? I don't need this partner any more. I am so happy with where I am and who I am, the need for this other is not there. Because I am the Beloved. I am so complete exactly where I am.

These patterns that had run my life are now complete. I am showing up differently in my life, and that is essentially what transformation is about. I no longer am alone. I reach out for help when I need it. I connect with others. I take time every day for me in self-care. I meditate, exercise, and talk, text, or email with at least one sister every day. I sing and dance inside my house, walk outside and touch trees. And of course, I listen. The other day I was driving in my car and my Grandmother came to me. She said, "Thank you." I knew what she meant. In my quest for finding happiness, I have learned not only to connect with the depths of myself, but I have also cleared the Field in my small way for others to follow. It is my heart's desire to have others know this infinite love and live with it every day, not just for a moment, but for this life and their lifetimes to come.

I read a beautiful analogy the other day from the same teacher who wrote the email when I was on Maui. He told the story of trying to navigate life on the open seas with a tiny rowboat. In the beginning, that is where I was. Not only did every little swell toss me around, but just a medium wave would throw me overboard. What I needed was a bigger boat. The storms and waves of life will always be there, but now I can navigate them so much more easily because I have this huge ocean liner traveling across the seas. I developed that bigger boat by spending time every day with Spirit, increasing the depths of my soul, listening, and paying attention to where I needed to go next. Not only did I learn to navigate the river, I entered the Ocean and the expansiveness of this new realm.

I heard a line in a song the other day and it said, "If love is not the answer, you are asking the wrong question." In my process of rediscovering my heart and opening it to this World, I have found that not only is love the answer, but self-love is our true essence. I have broken the patterns of being alone, and in that discovery,

I have come to know that I am. I will continue to have self-doubt and moments of confusion, but the unwavering love of this Universe is anchored deep within me and will help me navigate the next steps. I have found Heaven on Earth. I have come Home.

CONCLUSION

This book was written through me in about seven hours. The words just flowed, and I was along for the ride. I remember as I was writing that something special was happening, and I was happy to be playing with Spirit.

In preparing the book for publishing, I met another angel along the path, Lynn. She reflected back to me how there was a process she saw that had played out through this journey: divinely-led stages that had specific steps. She helped me see how these seasons that I went through had shaped and led me to realizing my true destiny.

This destiny journey was then put into language, and I gained clarity on who I am here to serve. It is the woman who is having this desire to move forward in her life but not necessarily knowing the steps on how to get there.

For that woman, you understand there is a force greater than yourself that can help you follow your path if you only let it guide you. It is my life purpose to help you connect with this wisdom, clarity and knowledge so that you can fulfill your destiny in this lifetime and all that you are meant to accomplish.

This distinct process that revealed itself is contained within the word DESTINY and mirrors each season as you've just read throughout the book:

D - Desire, Early Winter: This stage illustrates the yearning we have that burns inside us for something more, or something we've let lie hidden and haven't had the courage to face, and it is through this desire that we being to wake up and get ready to evolve to the next level.

E - Embrace, Winter: When I chose this path, all my old ways of being showed up, and I needed to face what wasn't working for me in my life. When you embrace it ALL, that is your first step to freedom, and that will allow you to take on this higher-level path.

S - Spirit-led, Spring: There is a power greater than us which I had always known, but I had not realized the extent of how it could anchor, lead, and guide me. The wisdom that can come through is far greater than what we can imagine for ourselves, and frankly, way better. In this stage, you allow yourself to feel the connection to guidance and stay open to what is put on your path.

T - Trust, Summer: Now you're getting into practice with all you are experiencing. Staying in trust will challenge old paradigms and test your comfort zone as you take on new experiences and understandings unknown to you before. This stage requires you to open even more to all – even when it seems like it is not turning out the way you initially hoped.

I - Intuition, Fall: Here is where I could step all the way into my inner knowing. In this stage you have to let old patterns fall away that aren't in alignment, allow the pain to flow through as you anchor more into what you know to be true, and fully own your power of trusting this inner knowing that there is something even greater waiting for you.

N - Next Steps, Winter: Life comes full circle and now new challenges and new experiences are revealing themselves. You can navigate through them with new ways of being, no longer being held back by old patterns. This path shifts your relationship to seeing challenges as opportunities. Now you ask the Universe, "What Next?" and stay in that trusting, aligned, intuitive place that's being led by Spirit.

Y- YOU, Spring: This is the glorious space when you experience yourself as whole and complete – exactly as you are. You feel the joy, freedom, and fulfillment of knowing your purpose, feeling alive and flowing abundantly with life, experiencing the full breadth of all that is available to you.

You are enough, you know enough, and you are ready to move into this yearning that is calling you forth.

You can actualize these potentials that are rising within and move them into action and vision and clarity.

Your time is now, and we are the ones we've been waiting for.

I so look forward to meeting you on the path.

Made in United States
North Haven, CT
17 February 2023

32782527R00031